# DADDY,
# WE HARDLY
# KNEW YOU

ALSO BY GERMAINE GREER

*The Female Eunuch*
*The Obstacle Race*
*Sex and Destiny*
*Shakespeare*
*The Madwoman's Underclothes*
*Kissing the Rod (ed.)*